GANDHI'S HINDUISM
The Struggle Against
JINNAH'S ISLAM

GANDHI'S HINDUISM
The Struggle Against
JINNAH'S ISLAM

M.J. AKBAR

BLOOMSBURY
NEW DELHI • LONDON • OXFORD • NEW YORK • SYDNEY

BLOOMSBURY INDIA
Bloomsbury Publishing India Pvt. Ltd
Second Floor, LSC Building No. 4, DDA Complex, Pocket C – 6 & 7,
Vasant Kunj, New Delhi 110070

BLOOMSBURY, BLOOMSBURY INDIA and the Diana logo are
trademarks of Bloomsbury Publishing Plc

First published in 2020
This paperback edition published 2022

Images courtesy: Nehru Memorial Museum & Library

ISBN PB: 978-93-94701-07-6; ebook: 978-93-89449-16-7

2 4 6 8 10 9 7 5 3 1

Printed and bound in India

To find out more about our authors and books, visit
www.bloomsbury.com and sign up for our newsletters

For Mallika,
head and heart
of my beloved family

Contents

Acknowledgments

The term 'professional' has acquired some sombre undertones. The high priests of corporate behaviour, one hears, switch off their smiles on the early Monday bird to office, and not a flicker returns until spirits are refuelled the following weekend. What a pleasure it was to meet executives from Bloomsbury, and find that they combine a gentle, warm demeanour with careful professionalism in the difficult and demanding business of publishing. I am very grateful to Paul Vinay Kumar, who nurtured this book through the publishing process, and Rajiv Beri, managing director of Bloomsbury for their belief and commitment. My enormous gratitude to Prabir Bambhal, a friend of many decades and now *eminence grise* of Indian publishing, for being the shepherd towards publication. Meenakshi Singh produced a splendid marketing plan; Saon Bhattacharya and Manisha Sobhrajani worked diligently and hard checking the manuscript: thank you.

Writing is a lonely occupation; I do not have the words to describe how much of a strength my wife Mallika has been, along with my sister Ghazala and brother-in-law Lokesh; they created a cocoon of love along with our children Mukulika and Carl, Prayaag and Shanta, and their three joyous boys, Julian, Kayan and Agastya. My family has been a bulwark: Sajda, Wajda, Saadat, Hasnain, Sibtain, Arif and others in Telinipara and elsewhere. The closest friends are those visible both in the gleam of festive phases and the gloom of tough times. I have received extraordinary and sustaining affection from Sunil, Geeta, Habib, Tony, Ajit Bhai, Tapan, Prasanna, Raian, Bharat, Arif, Anil, Veenu, Devesh, Subhash, Rani, Gopal, Mohandas, Satish, Virendra, SM, Ram, Rajiv, Naresh, Suman, Sandip and so many others from the lasting club of school pals and the various passages of a multiple-career life. A heartfelt bow to all. Thank you, my friends.

A final word of deep gratitude to a book's family: readers.

1

'Why I Am Proud to Be a Hindu'

Mohandas Karamchand Gandhi, architect of India's liberation from British rule, wanted to spend 15 August 1947, the first day of freedom, in breakaway Pakistan rather than in India. This was neither tokenism nor a gesture of support for a country carved out of multifaith India in the name of one religion, Islam. It was a promise of defiance. Gandhi simply did not believe in the partition of India, and the creation of new, 'unnatural' borders by an arbitrary scalpel in a fit of what he described as momentary madness. His immediate concern was the fate of partition's principal victims, the minorities: Hindus in Pakistan and Muslims in India. He wanted to be in Noakhali, East Pakistan, where Hindus had suffered bitterly in the 1946 riots and prevent any recurrence. Gandhi was still struggling to build hope from the incendiary debris of communal violence.

For over three decades of continuous struggle on the subcontinent, Gandhi had pursued a clear mission: the freedom and unity of India. Freedom had come, but at the cost of unity. India was split along its most vulnerable fault line, Hindu–Muslim differences. No one had fought the revanchist concept of an Islamic Pakistan with more conviction and consistency than Gandhi; no one had challenged its synthetic fallacies with more tenacity. For him, faith was harmony; how could it lead to such cruel discord? Gandhi's pride in Hinduism lay in its philosophy of tolerance. He could not fathom why an Indian Muslim needed to be in a different country to remain a Muslim; freedom of faith was cardinal to India's ethos, a principle that would become a constitutional commitment in united India. Gandhi had not won freedom from the British in order to deny freedom to Indians. What new rights could a theocratic idea like Pakistan offer to Indian Muslims?

By the summer of 1947, however, Gandhi knew that between the violence of faith supremacists, the helplessness of Congress leaders he had nurtured, and some careful British manipulation, he had lost the argument. But he refused to abandon his convictions. He had been betrayed by politics, but his moral certitude never wavered. On 31 May 1947, Gandhi told an ideological brother, the Pathan leader Abdul Ghaffar Khan, known as 'Frontier Gandhi', that he wanted to visit the North West Frontier and live in Pakistan after independence:

> [F]or I don't believe in these divisions of the country. I am not going to ask anybody's permission. If they kill me for their defiance, I shall embrace death with a smiling face. That is, if Pakistan comes into existence, I intend to go there, tour it, live there and see what they do to me.[1]

He also foresaw the terrible consequences of partition. On 20 July 1947, after the date of independence had been formally announced, Gandhi said in a prayer meeting in New Delhi:

> I cannot rejoice on 15 August. I do not want to deceive you ... India's partition has grieved me more than it could grieve you.... Unfortunately the freedom we have got today contains also the seeds of future conflict between India and Pakistan. How can we therefore light the lamps?[2]

The ferocity of that 'future conflict' became visible in riots and war at the very outset. Massacres accompanied partition, and in October 1947, Pakistan started a hybrid war where the formal engagement of armies was overwhelmed by barbaric terrorism. Over more than seven decades, that 'future conflict' has become the longest continual war in known history.

Gandhi inherited his inclusive, embracing faith from his mother, Putlibai. She belonged to a Hindu sect known as Pranami, which practised what it preached: that all religions emerged from the same eternal being. Its scripture regarded the Muslim Quran to be as divine as the Hindu Vedas. Her syncretic values left an abiding, deep and lifelong influence on her son.

Gandhi was born on 2 October 1869 in a hundred-year-old, three-storey house, the residence of officials who had served the small Princely States of Kathiawar in Gujarat for six generations. Their means did not permit extravagance, but neither were they indigent. As Modh Banias, they belonged to a caste within the upper echelons of Hindu hierarchy. His grandfather, Uttamchand (or Ota) Gandhi, had risen to become the diwan, or premier, of Porbandar. When he fell out with the princess regent, Rani Rupaliba, her troops attacked the Gandhi home. An Arab bodyguard protected Ota Gandhi. Gandhi's father, Karamchand (known as Kaba), born in 1822, was appointed, in succession, the diwan of three Princely States—Porbandar, Rajkot and Wankaner. Putlibai, Kaba's fourth wife, was less than half his age; the previous three had died, two in childbirth. Kaba viewed his work as a combination of administrative responsibility and social duty. There might have been as many as twenty guests for dinner on a regular basis, but Kaba did help out by peeling vegetables, while Putlibai took charge of the kitchen.

Gandhi admired his father's professional integrity and his mother's piety. 'The outstanding impression my mother has left on my memory is that of saintliness. She was deeply religious,' he writes in his autobiography. His father was incorruptible, with a reputation for impartiality and loyalty to the state, but not particularly orthodox. Instead, '...he had that kind of religious culture which frequent visits to temples and listening to religious discourses make available to many Hindus.'[3]

His mother's influence prevailed. Gandhi recalls that even though they were Hindu by birth, their Pranami temple priest used to read from both the Gita and the Quran, moving from one to the other, as if it did not matter which book was being read as long as God was being worshipped.

The Pranami Sampradaya, founded in the 17th century by Devchandra Maharaj (1581–1655), emerged during an era when the transformative policies of Mughal emperor Akbar were energising the expanding Mughal domain with a new amity between the predominantly Hindu population and a largely Muslim ruling elite. Devchandra came from Umarkot, coincidentally the place where Akbar was born during his father Humayun's years of exile in the Sindh desert. At sixteen, Devchandra renounced the world in search of *Brahma-gyan* (knowledge of Brahma, the Supreme God). He settled down in Jamnagar, called his followers Nijanand Sampradaya, or the Self-Awakening Sect, and divine knowledge *Tartam*. Its doctrine of Hindu–Muslim harmony is captured by this couplet: *Jo kachu kahya Ved ne, so hi kahya Kitab/Donon bandey ek Sahib ke, par larhat paya bina bhed* (That which is said in the Vedas, is also said in the Book [Quran]/ Both are children of One God, but quarrel without knowing the truth).

Devchandra's most important disciple, Mahamati Prannathji (1618–94), travelled to Oman, Iran and Iraq, and compiled the Pranami Dharma's scripture, Kuljam Swaroop. It incorporates passages from the Vedas, Bhagavad Gita, Quran, Bible and Torah.[4] Honouring various religious sentiments, the sect prohibits alcohol, meat and tobacco. There are no idols in Pranami temples. With typical Indian inclusiveness, Gandhi's mother worshipped at Hindu temples, revered Jain monks and practised their traditions like fasting. She would, recalled Gandhi, '...take the hardest vows and keep them without flinching.... Living on one meal a day during *Chaturmas*[5] was a habit with her.'[6] On days when she vowed not to eat without seeing the sun, and abstain even if the sky was clouded, her worried son would stand outside, searching for a glimpse of sunshine so that he could tell his mother to break her fast. It is easy to trace the origin of Gandhi's own deep commitment to fasting, which he developed both as a penance and a political weapon, to his mother.

When Gandhi became the leader of India's freedom movement, his prayer meetings began with recitations from all major scriptures. He included the opening chapter of the Quran, the *Surah Fatehah*, in praise of the *Rab al Alamin*, or Lord of the Universe, alongside the litany of multifaith prayers in his ashram.[7] The psychoanalyst Erik Erikson, who wrote a unique, if controversial, biography of the boy who became a Mahatma, comments:

> His mother's religion was of that pervasive and personalized kind which women convey to children; but it also prepared the boy for the refusal to take anybody's word for what anything meant, either in the Hindu scriptures which he rediscovered only in his youth with the help of Western writings, or in the Christian gospels, the essence of which he tried to resurrect in Eastern and modern terms...[8]

The natural tendency of a child, Gandhi notes, is to learn about faith by 'picking up things here and there from my surroundings'[9]. His nurse, Rambha, told him to ward off ghosts by reciting the name of Lord Rama, and ensure all-day protection by reciting the *Rama Raksha* verse each morning after his bath. Gandhi rather enjoyed the visible obligations of his caste, such as a *shikha* (or knot) in his hair, and yearned to wear the holy thread meant only for Brahmins. The broad family mind narrowed in one aspect. Gandhi was forbidden any contact at home with the 'untouchable'[10] boy who came to clean the latrines. This injustice troubled the young Gandhi and raised questions that would later evolve into a core reformist mission within Hinduism.

Gandhi recalls that his bedridden father's Parsi and Muslim friends would visit and discuss religion. The teenage Gandhi, nursing his ill parent, listened and learnt. A priest called Ladha Maharaj came to recite melodious *dohas* (couplets) and *chopais* (quatrains) from the Ramayana, inspiring an early love for what Gandhi would later describe as the 'greatest book in all devotional literature'[11]. Lord Rama became Gandhi's ideal hero, although it was the Gita, from Hinduism's defining war epic, Mahabharata, which became the more influential text. Gandhi described the Gita as his *Dharma Grantha*, or spiritual dictionary, a mirror for one's inner self and a lodestar for one's actions. It dealt with the 'invisible' war, the moral conflict, which was so much more difficult than any physical conflict. Courage was not violence; true courage was non-violence. The defining principle of Gita, action without attachment, was possible only through non-violence or Ahimsa. Non-violence did not emerge out of fear of violence. As he wrote in *Hind Swaraj,* if he ceased stealing because of fear of punishment, he would return to theft the moment that fear disappeared.

The absence of attachment led to a dissolution of the ego. Gandhi learnt *Stithatprajna*, the ability to remain calm when engaged in the most turbulent strife, from the Gita. The war in Mahabharata was an allegory to teach great truths, which could be applied in normal existence; for Gandhi, religion was not religion until it met the needs of the 'hurly-burly of everyday life'. The Gita was a sacred text precisely because it was a gospel of daily existence.

His own life was, as the title of his autobiography aptly puts it, a continuous experiment with truth; and truth was synonymous with religion. His Hinduism was the realisation of the permanent from the evanescent, in the spirit of Advaita philosophy. Both his private and public life were epitomised by struggle: the first to reach the highest expression of faith and the second to cleanse India of foreign rule. The strength he found in the former enabled him to pursue the latter.

His personal behaviour drew from the values enunciated in the Upanishads: *dama* (self-control), *tapas* (self-discipline), *mauna* (silence), *dana* (sharing), *daya* (benevolence) and *brahmacharya* (celibacy). As Dr S. Radhakrishnan explains in *The Principal Upanishads*, dama means reducing our wants to the minimal; overcoming anger and lust in the mind (*krodham samena jayati, kamam samkalpa-varjanat/sattva-samsevanad dhiro nidram ucchettum arhati*: Brahma Purana 235, 40). 'Austerity, chastity, solitude and silence are the ways to attain self-control,' writes Dr Radhakrishnan. The purpose of tapas is spiritual, achieved through the elimination of natural desires and distractions of the outer world, till you arrive at the tranquillity of renunciation. Silence (or mauna) leads the soul to contemplation, curbing excesses of the tongue like flattery or backbiting. Dana is not merely generosity; it is freedom from acquisition. You cannot seek God while sitting on a throne. Daya, or *karuna*, is compassion; at peace with all through forgiveness. Brahmacharya (celibacy) is strength as well as beauty: sex is needed only to plant a seed for the creation of another body for the presence of a soul; excess destroys one's body and brain. Gandhi practised each of these principles, even at the cost of being misunderstood, particularly when, towards the end of his life, he insisted on an experiment with celibacy to the shock of friends, the horror of followers, the bewilderment of sympathisers and the amazement of foes. He abandoned privacy completely.

He sought the ultimate tranquillity: to envy no one, to possess nothing, to fear none, to desire nothing. Detachment was something more than renunciation from the world; it was involvement for a higher purpose. The moral power sustained his credibility even when contradictions threatened to tar his reputation.

Gandhi preferred to emphasise the inclusive element in other faiths.[12] In Islam, for instance, God is described as *Rab al Aalameen*, or the God of the whole universe, and not as *Rab al Muslimeen*, or the God of Muslims. How we worship that same eternal being is our option, which we must exercise without fear or hindrance.

He generally spoke for about fifteen minutes at his prayer meetings on whichever subject he felt merited attention. On 30 May 1947, he said in New Delhi:

> I was born a Hindu. No one can undo the fact. But I am also a Muslim because I am a good Hindu. In the same way I am also a Parsi and Christian too. At the basis of all religions there is the name of only one God. All the scriptures say the same thing.[13]

He, who found comfort and inspiration in the fact that all those who had given the world great religions were selfless, was deeply impressed by Prophet Muhammad's asceticism when he first read about the founder of Islam in Thomas Carlyle's *Heroes and Hero Worship*. The central challenge of his political life was the relationship between Hindus and Muslims; he sought harmony from the Quran, not conflict. He refused to share the view that the Quran had given Muslims some divine right to kill 'infidels'. He could not totally deny those verses, which urged jihad or holy war, but he had a persuasive explanation: the Quran preached non-violence as a duty and violence only as a necessity. He remarked, astutely, that Muhammad had accepted suffering and humiliation in Mecca before he left for Medina to establish a state. In any case, it was not his intention to judge Islam's or Christianity's[14] prophet; his belief in non-violence was independent of any scripture.

Gandhi was always ready to substantiate claim through experience and example. For instance, when questioned about war and Islam, he recalled the time he had spent during the 1946 riots, saving Muslims in Bihar and protecting Hindus at Noakhali in Bengal.

> No Bihari Muslim told me that since I was a non-believer they would kill me. Nor did the Maulvis[15] in Noakhali say any such thing. On the contrary, they allowed the *Ramadhun*[16] to the accompaniment of the *dholak*[17]. All that the Koran says is that the infidel would be answerable to God. But God would demand an explanation from everyone, even from a Muslim. And He would not question you about your words but your deeds. But then those who are keen on seeing dirt can find it everywhere. There is nothing in which good and bad are not mixed up. Why, our Manusmriti[18] talks of pouring molten lead into the ears of the 'untouchables'[19]! But I would say that that is not the true teaching of our [Hindu] scriptures. Tulsidas[20] gives the essence of all Shastras in his statement that compassion is the root of all religions. No religion ever teaches us to kill anyone.

He continued his increasingly forlorn plea to prevent what, on 30 May 1947, seemed inevitable: 'We must make it clear that even if we all have to die or the whole country is reduced to ashes, Pakistan will not be conceded under duress.'[21]

Equality of faith was fundamental to Gandhi's vision of a united India. Since no faith was superior, conversion was unnecessary or irrelevant. This neatly excised a major source of tension between religious communities. Conversion was forbidden in his ashram. He gave his devoted English disciple, Madeline Slade, whom he called a daughter, the name Mirabehn, but never allowed her to change her Christian religion. Her new name was Indian, he explained, not Hindu. While at school, he writes in his autobiography, 'I sort of developed a dislike for it [Christianity]. And for a reason. In those days Christian missionaries used to stand in a corner near the high school and hold forth, pouring abuse on Hindus and their gods. I could not endure this.'[22]

He was, as ever, consistent, whatever the time or context. In 1921, when he learnt that some Moplah Muslims in Kerala had forced Hindus to convert during communal riots, he called it 'tyranny' and 'terrorism'[23]. The anthropologist Prof. Nirmal Bose recalls that on 25 November 1946, Gandhi told Bengali Muslims who had attacked a Hindu temple in Noakhali, 'The Prophet [Muhammad] once advised Mussulmans [sic] to consider the Jewish places of worship to be as pure as their own, and offer it the same protection.'[24] For Gandhi, Hinduism represented an embracing and ethical way of life; the depressing and often demeaning rituals that it had acquired were an accretion imposed by human beings. But he promoted reform not with the disgust of an English lord demanding a ban on suttee, but as a deeply pious Hindu for whom such behaviour was a wretched deviation from a moral path that stretched back to the Upanishads. Social malpractice was an impurity, an alienation from the real truth of Hinduism, an assertion of base human desire against God's universal will.

GOD AND SATYAGRAHA

The seminal moment in Gandhi's evolution as a radical and unique political philosopher and activist came during his two decades in South Africa.

The first Indians arrived in South Africa as indentured labour for Natal's plantations in the 1860s. In 1893, with a change in the political structure, the rights of Indians began to be pared; in 1896, they were disenfranchised. Gandhi was twenty-three when he was hired as an attorney by a Muslim businessman, Dada Abdullah, for a modest fee of 105 pounds plus first-class return fare. He expected to stay for a year at the very most; but he remained for twenty-one years. His legal acumen was, very soon, less in demand than his exceptional courage and extraordinary leadership. He became the face and voice of the Indian struggle for legitimate rights.

Dutch-origin Boers had dominated the region for over two hundred years, but by the end of the 19th century, after two wars, they had lost out to the ever-expanding British Empire. Britain paid a heavy price in the Second Boer War between October 1899 and May 1902. The British had to put 400,000 men in the field under their most experienced commander, General Lord Kitchener, and suffered over 22,000 dead and more than 75,000 wounded before they prevailed. The Treaty of Vereeniging ensured self-government to Transvaal (South African Republic) and Orange Free State, but as British colonies. The Boers were co-opted into the Empire.

Indians, expecting better treatment from British rule, discovered that their situation had deteriorated. In 1906, the authorities decided to restrict Indian immigration. Among new measures was the introduction of permits with a signature or thumb impression, later embellished with a photograph, without which residence would be illegal. An Asiatic Bill was proposed. Indians condemned it (without irony) as the Black Act, and Gandhi saw nothing in the draft except hatred for Indians. On 8 September 1906, Gandhi sent a cable to Lord Minto, the viceroy of India, describing this bill as a 'degrading, insulting' ordinance which 'reduces Indians to a worse status than that of pariahs'. He requested the viceroy's intervention since the latter was 'directly responsible for their welfare'[25]. Calcutta, then the capital of the British Raj, was impervious. On 11 September 1906, some 3,000 anxious Indians, both Hindu and Muslim, gathered at the Empire Theatre in Johannesburg. Abdul Gani, chairman of the Transvaal British Indian Association, was in the chair. Sheth Haji Habib made an impassioned plea to pass a resolution against this law, with God as the witness. It was the first time, Gandhi recalls, that he had heard God being mentioned in such a political context; he was taken aback by Sheth Habib's suggestion of an oath, but warmly approved of it. He stood up to explain what this meant.

'We all believe in one and the same God,' said Gandhi, 'the differences of nomenclature in Hinduism and Islam notwithstanding. To pledge ourselves or to take an oath in the name of that God or with Him as witness is not something to be trifled with.' He explained that '...there is a vast difference between this resolution and every other resolution we have passed to date.' This was the acid test. He warned that they could face jail, hunger, hard labour, flogging and penury but could not resort to either violence or 'internal violence' against the oppressor. Their cause was just, their means morally pure and victory was inevitable: 'I can boldly declare, and with certainty, that so long as there is even a handful of men true to their pledge, there can be only one end to the struggle, and that is victory'.[26] The next day, in an accident, the theatre was destroyed by fire. The Indians took this as a welcome omen. The ordinance would meet the fate of the theatre.

That speech marked the launch of a doctrine that by 1947 would undermine the British Raj in India and, in consequence, end the age of British and European colonialism. Gandhi, after much thought, named this Satyagraha, a civil disobedience movement anchored in *satya* (truth), *agraha* (firmness) and *ahimsa* (non-violence), wrapped in yet another brilliant departure from conventional confrontation—empathy for the oppressor. The objective was to transform the foe into seeing the error of his ways, not to defeat him.

The movement was first described as passive resistance, but Gandhi, who had witnessed such a strategy in England, wanted a unique Indian term for a unique Indian path. This was much more than passive resistance, which Gandhi considered both weak and morally inadequate, since it had the potential of being clouded by hatred. 'As the struggle advanced,' he writes, 'the phrase "passive resistance" gave rise to confusion and it appeared shameful to permit this great struggle to be known only by an English name.'[27] A reader of Gandhi's journal in South Africa, *Indian Opinion,* suggested 'Sada-graha', or firmness in a good cause. Gandhi liked the word, but not enough. He altered it to 'Satyagraha'. 'Truth [Satya] implies love and firmness [Agraha] engenders, and therefore serves as a synonym for force,' he wrote in *Satyagraha in South Africa*. This was a non-violent soul force and brute force had no place in it, in any circumstance. Satyagraha was gentle, it never wounded, it could never be violent. 'A *Satyagrahi*,' writes Dennis Dalton, 'concentrates on the common interest and strives not for retribution but to transform a conflict situation so that warring parties can come out of a confrontation convinced that it was in their mutual interest to do so.'[28]

Always willing to recognise truth wherever he found it, Gandhi recalls that he first witnessed the spirit of Satyagraha during the Second Boer War. Not in Boer men, who were ever ready to fight, but in the courage of the women. He writes in *Satyagraha in South Africa*:

> [Boer women] understood that their religion required them to suffer in order to preserve their independence, and therefore patiently and cheerfully endured all hardships. Lord Kitchener[29] left no stone unturned in order to break their spirit. He confined them in separate concentration camps, where they suffered indescribable sufferings. They starved, they suffered biting cold and scorching heat. Sometimes a soldier intoxicated with liquor or maddened by passion might even assault these

> unprotected women. Still the brave Boer women did not flinch. And at last, King Edward [of Britain] wrote to Lord Kitchener, saying that he could not tolerate it, and that if it was the only means of reducing the Boers to submission, he would prefer any sort of peace to continuing the war in that fashion, and asking the General to bring the war to a speedy end.... Real suffering bravely borne melts even a heart of stone. Such is the potency of suffering, or *tapas.* And there lies the key to Satyagraha.[30]

Gandhi, deeply impressed by Jesus' Sermon on the Mount, truly believed that the meek would inherit the earth, and that turning the other cheek paid dividends in the rather less sacred field of practical politics.

Gandhi's first Satyagraha lasted eight years. Its climax came in 1913, in a confrontation that caught the imagination of the world, and eventually the respect of Boer heroes, Louis Botha, then first prime minister of the Union of South Africa[31], and Jan Christiaan Smuts, then minister of defence and native affairs, who rose to become president of South Africa in 1939, field marshal and a friend of Britain's legendary prime minister, Winston Churchill. A great moment of vindication came in 1913 when the viceroy of India, Lord Hardinge, spoke out, not on behalf of his Empire compatriots, but in favour of Gandhi. Gandhi surely remembered how, at the start of his Satyagraha in 1906, he had been rebuffed by a previous viceroy, Lord Minto. The circumstances that drove the Satyagraha towards its decisive phase were most unusual.

In 1908, a resident of Port Elizabeth, Hassan Esop, visited India and married Bai Mariam. She did not accompany him when he returned in 1909. She came to join him in 1912, but the immigration officer refused admission. On 14 March 1913, Justice Malcolm Searle of the Cape Supreme Court passed an order confirming her expulsion on the grounds that the Muslim marriage law, which permitted polygamy and was legal in British India, was not valid in South Africa. There was an uproar, as Hindu law permitted polygamy as well at that time.

Gandhi took up the cause, writing in the *Indian Opinion* of 22 March 1913, 'The meaning of the judgement is that every Hindu and Mohammedan wife is in South Africa illegally, and, therefore, at the mercy of the Government, whose grace alone can enable her to remain in the country.' If the marriage was illegal, then wives were technically concubines, and children, being illegitimate, could not claim inheritance rights. The social and economic structure of Indian society was under threat. On 30 March, Gandhi told a meeting of Indians at the Hamidia Islamic Society's Hall in Johannesburg that they must prepare for resistance in defence of 'womanhood and its honour'[32].

In September, Gandhi prepared to put his 'army of peace' into battle once again; but this time its most potent soldier would be his own wife, Kasturbai, also known as Kasturba. He and Kasturbai Makhanji Kapadia were wed in 1882, when he was fourteen and she was more than six months older, then the conventional age for arranged marriages. Kasturba was incensed when she heard that according to this new law for Indians, she was no longer legally Gandhi's wife. In that case, she said, they should return to India. Gandhi replied that it would be cowardly to do so. 'Could I not, then, join the struggle and be imprisoned myself?' Kasturba asked. Gandhi warned that the process would be hard, her health was poor, and she could not weaken once the hardships mounted. Kasturba refused to relent. Inspired, other women at Phoenix, where she lived, offered to join her.

On 15 September, a small band of four women, including Kasturba, and twelve men took the Kafir[33] Mail from Durban, travelling third class and taking only the bare essentials. At Volksrust, they were arrested for crossing the border without a permit, deported on 22 September and rearrested when they tried to cross again. They were sentenced between one and three months' hard labour in Maritzburg jail, where they were given appalling food and harsh laundry work.

Gandhi began his Satyagraha on 25 September with two demands: recognition of marriages and repeal of a punitive tax of three pounds for former indentured labour who wanted to work again. The arrest of the women had an immediate impact. Indian coalminers at Newcastle went on strike. Gandhi met them on 20 October and heard how miners had been beaten and driven out of their homes. There was little money, even for food, but the miners joined Gandhi like 'pilgrims', along with their wives and children, bringing nothing but a meagre bundle upon their heads. Rations were reduced to a pound-and-a-half of bread, and an ounce of sugar. Gandhi wrote in the *Indian Opinion* of 20 October 1913, with some satisfaction, that men were taking orders from women without argument.

On 21 October, more women were sentenced to hard labour after proudly admitting their 'guilt'. On 28 October, Gandhi began a march of the impoverished from Newcastle to his Tolstoy Farm, where he thought he might be able to provide better sustenance. The march became news. Newspapers reported that his emaciated followers were calling Gandhi 'Bapu' or father. According to D.G. Tendulkar, *The Times,* London, reported, '...that the march of the Indian labourers, must live in memory as one of the most remarkable manifestations in the history of the spirit of passive resistance.'[34] If England was touched, India was stirred. India's national poet, Rabindranath Tagore, sent a letter to Gandhi praising this ascent 'not through the bloody path of violence but that of dignified patience and heroic self-renunciation'[35].

Gandhi was arrested en route, but the march continued. On 11 November, Gandhi was sentenced to either a fine of 60 pounds or nine months of rigorous imprisonment. Naturally, Gandhi opted for the second. Thousands were also in jail by now and anger in India rose to outrage, particularly at the harsh treatment of the imprisoned women. Protests were sent to the viceroy, Lord Hardinge. On 27 December, Hardinge announced that he would send a senior civil servant, Sir Benjamin Robertson, to assist Indians in South Africa. Donations to the South African Resistance Fund began to swell, including from princes.

The South African government had begun to wilt. An Indian Grievances Commission was set up on 11 December, but since two of its members were known for their bias against Indians, it did not raise much hope. On its recommendation, however, Gandhi was released on 18 December, whereupon which he promptly announced another march for 1 January 1914. He thought some 5,000 would join; over 20,000 came. Botha and Smuts were also under pressure from friends in London, who had been sympathetic to the Boer cause. Hearts were changing, as Gandhi always said they would during a Satyagraha.

Gandhi was persuaded to postpone his march by a fortnight. Suddenly, barriers began to crumble. Smuts called Gandhi for talks and they met on 9 January. Letters were exchanged. On 21 January, there was a provisional agreement, which was signed the next day. The Satyagraha was over. The Indians' Relief Bill legalised all Sharia and Hindu marriages; the three-pound tax was abolished. In June, Gandhi wrote to Smuts saying that a chapter that had commenced in September 1906 was finally closed.

When Gandhi sailed for home from Durban on 18 July 1914, Smuts remarked, 'The Saint has left our shores, I sincerely hope for ever.'[36] The 'Saint' had other plans. He had also acquired a holy name: the people called him 'Mahatma' or great soul.

Smuts was more impressed by Gandhi than he cared to admit in 1914. This became known nearly three decades later. We learn from the diaries of Lord Moran, Churchill's personal physician, that Smuts was dining with Churchill in London on 7 August 1942. The news of the day was Gandhi's call to the British at a Congress session in Bombay to 'Quit India' and his message to Indians: 'Do or die!' Smuts told Churchill never to underestimate Gandhi: 'He is a man of God. You and I are mundane people. Gandhi has appealed to religious motives. You never have. That is *where you have failed.*' Churchill replied, 'with a grin', 'I have made more bishops than anyone since St. Augustine.'[37] Smuts remained grave.

Arthur Herman, who quotes this exchange in *Gandhi & Churchill: The Epic Rivalry That Destroyed an Empire and Forged Our Age*, writes:

> What Smuts the philosopher could see, and Churchill could not, was the Mahatma's supreme spirituality, which had made him revered across India and even in the West. It was a power that few other understood. Most in Gandhi's own inner circle had given up trying. Instead, they had learned to obey it as a matter of principle. Others followed simply as a matter of instinct, as if in obedience to a natural leader ... [Gandhi's conception of life] rested on a vision of spiritual purity in which history and material things (including Gandhi's own body) counted for nothing.... [Gandhi] valued liberty as *God's* supreme achievement. It was man's duty to live up to that standard. Without it, Gandhi believed, life was meaningless, including his own.[38]

THE RAJ AND RELIGION

After the great 1857 uprising, the British were convinced about the potent political unity that faith could inspire in the subcontinent they had subdued. They also set about, carefully, to use it to their advantage.

They invested in a more cynical use of religion, to divide Indians along faith-identity, a perfectly logical option for an imperial power. They turned it into a weapon against an incipient and, in their view, unrealistic Indian nationalism. Their policies, aimed understandably at self-preservation, now sought to exploit the seams of faith, offering social or economic advantages through religious and sectional compartments, encouraging competition between Indians that could, at the throw of a statute, be escalated into conflict. In 1905, the Raj partitioned its most important province, Bengal, on Hindu–Muslim lines in support of this thesis. In 1909, through the Indian Councils Act, they increased the participation of Indians in the legislature, but included a provision unique to any voting system. Only Muslims were given the right to elect Muslims through separate electorates. This split the political ethos, for it was based on the assumption that Hindus could not be trusted with Muslim interests. A communal infection, like a cancerous cell, had been planted at the source of political life.

At exactly the same time, Gandhi was promoting a more positive interpretation of religion as a force multiplier for unity, describing interfaith harmony as the modern idea. Gandhi wrote in the 26 August 1905 edition of *Indian Opinion*: 'The time has now passed, when the followers of one religion can stand and say, ours is the only true religion and all others are false. The growing spirit of toleration towards all religions is a happy augury of the future.' He praised a recent article in a London weekly, *The Christian World*, which argued that the '...world's religions are linked one with the other, each having characteristics common to all others.... Religion, by a hundred different names and forms, has been dropping the one seed into the human heart, opening the one truth as the mind was able to receive it.'[39] Gandhi had a specific message for India:

> To Europeans and Indians working together for the common good, this has special significance. India, with its ancient religions, has much to give, and the bond of unity between us can best be fostered by wholehearted sympathy and appreciation of each other's form of religion. A greater toleration of this important question would mean a wider charity in our everyday relations, and the existing misunderstandings would be swept away. Is it not also a fact that between Mahomedan [sic] and Hindu there is a great need for this toleration? Sometimes one is inclined to think it is even greater than between East and West. Let not strife and tumult destroy the harmony between Indians themselves. A house divided against itself must fall, so let me urge the necessity of perfect unity and brotherliness between all sections of the Indian community.[40]

When Gandhi returned home on 9 January 1915, he arrived with his principles tested in action, forged through arduous experience in conditions that could scarcely be more hostile. India's complexities did not shift the bookends of his philosophy, Satyagraha and Ahimsa.

The first of his three mass uprisings against British rule, called the non-cooperation or Khilafat movement, took place between 1920 and 1922. It was constructed on an alliance with Muslims who were emotionally distraught at the defeat of the last Muslim world power, the Turkish Caliphate, and consumed by the thought that with Jerusalem already in British hands, the two holy cities of Mecca and Medina would also be lost to the 'infidel'. Gandhi sympathised because he considered a brother's grief to be his own grief. More important, however, was the fact that Muslim rage was concentrated on the British.

Gandhi had one non-negotiable condition: non-violence. Muslim leaders agreed to follow his lead, although for many of them, this was a tactical compromise. Even in the heat of an amazing mass mobilisation, Gandhi was quite ready to chastise the most important of Muslim leaders who breached his non-violence marker, and ensure that both rhetoric and action remained on a non-violent trajectory. When a firebrand stalwart, Maulana Shaukat Ali, sought revenge against the British, on the basis of an 'eye for an eye', Gandhi pointed out that this would leave the whole world blind.

Gandhi's oath for Khilafat volunteers is an excellent example of what Judith Brown has described as 'religion in action'[41]. It reads:

> With God as witness we Hindus and Mahomedans [sic] declare that we shall behave towards one another as children of the same parents, that we shall have no differences, that the sorrows of each shall be the sorrows of the other and that each shall help the other in removing them. We shall respect each other's religion and religious feelings and shall not stand in the way of our respective religious practices. We shall always refrain from violence to each other in the name of religion.[42]

The British had enough personal and institutional experience of war. It has been noted that they were at war in some part of the world or the other through the whole of Queen Victoria's reign. More recently, a generation of youth had perished in the awesome bloodshed of the First World War. What bewildered them was non-violence, and its counterpart, non-cooperation.

Gandhi had honed his ideas about non-cooperation from the Gita. There were good men like Karna, Bhishma and Drona on the side of the Kauravas, he said, which suggested that evil could not survive or flourish without the support of some who were good. The British Raj, similarly, could not continue without the help of some good Indians. The purpose of non-cooperation was to remove such good Indians, both Hindus and Muslims, from the apparatus of British rule. If Hindus and Muslims united, they would become free; if they were divided, they would be slaves of the British.

Gandhi remained consistent through the long and turbulent roller-coaster ride of high-voltage events. For more than fifty years, he sang, literally, from the same hymn sheet. Religion, said his hymn, was a catechism of love, tolerance and unity. Whether in South Africa or India, for over half of a century till the end of his public career in 1948, he explained why he was proud to be a Hindu.

THE KINGDOM OF RAMA

On 21 November 1947, Gandhi began his prayer meeting speech in Delhi by extolling the virtues of cows' milk. He recalled the time in 1927 when, during an intense tour of southern India, he saw the 'best cow in the whole of Asia'[43], at a military dairy run by a certain Col William Smith in Bangalore. He then answered three questions from the audience, 'What is meant by "Hindu"? What is the origin of that word? Is there anything called Hinduism?'[44]

The term 'Hindu', he said, did not occur in the Vedas. The Greeks, under Alexander, coined it for people across the river Sindhu (Indus), changing the S into an H.

> The religion of the people living in this region [east of Indus] came to be known as Hinduism which, as you are well aware,

> is the most tolerant of religions. It gave shelter to the Christians who had escaped from the harassment of the people of other religions. Besides, it also gave shelter to the Jews known as Beni-Israel and also to the Parsis. I feel proud to belong to the Hinduism which embraces all religions and is very tolerant. The Aryan scholars followed the Vedic religion and India was first known as Aryavarta. I do not wish that once again the country should be known as Aryavarta. The Hinduism of my conception is complete in itself. Of course, it includes the Vedas, but it also includes many other things. I do not think it is improper to say that I can proclaim the same faith in the greatness of Islam, Christianity, Zoroastrianism and Judaism without in any way impairing the greatness of Hinduism. Such Hinduism would live so long as the sun shines in the sky.[45]

This did not mean that Gandhi accepted that Hinduism as then practised always reflected its essence. As a teenager, he had almost veered towards atheism after reading Manusmriti. Parallel to his politics ran a zeal to rid Hinduism of odious evils like 'untouchability', which he called satanic. Reform, he said, was necessary for the very survival of Hinduism. He became angry when water from a village well was denied to 'low castes', noting, acerbically, that a cow could drink this water but not a 'Sudra'.

What he did learn from religion, in his own words, was:

> [T]he conviction that morality is the basis of things, and that truth is the substance of all morality. Truth became my sole objective.... A Gujarati didactic stanza likewise gripped my mind and heart. Its precept—return good for evil—became my guiding principle. It became such a passion with me that I began numerous experiments in it. Here are those (for me) wonderful lines: *For a bowl of water give a goodly meal; For a kindly greeting bow thou down with zeal; For a simple penny pay thou back with gold; If thy life be rescued, life do not withhold. Thus the words and actions of the wise regard; Every little service tenfold they reward. But the truly noble know all men as one, And return with gladness good for evil done.*[46]

If Hinduism shaped Gandhi, then Gandhi also reformed Hinduism. The story of India's liberation from colonialism has subsumed the narrative of Gandhi's liberating impact on the internal fault lines of his faith.

His metaphor for a post-British utopia was 'Ramarajya'[47]. Through the freedom struggle, Gandhi promised Indians the peace and shared prosperity of Ramarajya. He used the term because peasants and farmers would quickly understand it as a definition of change, of a new order after freedom. God could only appear to the poor, said Gandhi, in the form of work; neither strife nor poverty had any place in Ramarajya. The blood and chaos that accompanied India's independence were the very antithesis of Ramarajya. On 19 October 1947, Gandhi lamented in Delhi:

> I admit that we have won it [freedom] on August 15. But I do not regard it as true Swaraj.[48] It is not the Swaraj of my conception. Nor can this Swaraj be called Ramarajya. Today we have come to regard each other as enemies. Muslims are enemies of the Hindus and the Hindus and the Sikhs are enemies of the Muslims. But Swaraj of my conception means that we do not want to regard anyone as our enemy, nor do we want to be enemies of anyone. That Swaraj has not yet come. Should the Hindus and the Muslims in India consider themselves enemies of each other? Will our brothers live in mutual animosity? ... The temple and the mosque are one and the same. Then why is it that the Muslims should destroy the temples and Hindus destroy the mosques? They are equally at fault in the eyes of God.... I have already said that I shall either do or die in Delhi.[49]

Those were fateful words.

2

A March Deal, an August Declaration

Mohammad Ali Jinnah, the single parent of Pakistan, was a Khoja Ismaili, a close-knit mercantile Shia community owing allegiance to the Aga Khan dynasty, whose ancestors had fled persecution in Persia and taken sanctuary in Gujarat. 'Khoja' is a Gujarati variation of the Persian honorific, 'Khwaja'. In a notable coincidence, the family had settled in Rajkot, about thirty miles south of where Gandhi was born. As a young entrepreneur, his father, Jinnahbhai Poonja, shifted to Karachi to take advantage of the economic boom that followed the opening of the Suez Canal in 1869, as trade shifted to the first commercial Indian port on the new sea route between Britain and its Indian Empire. Karachi was 200 miles closer than Bombay. Poonja prospered as an exporter and importer.

Jinnah was born in Karachi on 25 December 1876[1] and brought up in comfort. He had private tutors, a carriage to take him to the elite Christian Mission High School, played cricket and enjoyed riding. In 1893, after an early and brief marriage (his teenage wife died), he went to London, took up further studies, entered Lincoln's Inn and joined the bar in 1895. He settled in Bombay on his return, set up chambers and having established a reputation in court, initiated a parallel career in politics. In his twenties, Jinnah left the main branch of the Khoja Ismaili sect to join the smaller

Isna Ashari sect, which does not accept any leader. It seems to have been a sign of his temperament.

His first political strides were liberal. His lifestyle mirrored that of an Indian–English gentleman in dress, language, food and a secular indifference to religious practices, complemented by an excellent English accent and a taste for Scotch and Shakespeare. He preferred English to Gujarati, his mother tongue.

He was a moderate in Congress circles and ignored a new party created in 1906, the All India Muslim League, with British blessings and Sir Sultan Muhammad Shah, or Aga Khan III, the forty-eighth Imam of Khoja Ismailis, as its honorary president. The Aga Khan, also born in Karachi, was a year younger than Jinnah. Although obligations to his community required a peripatetic lifestyle and homes across the globe, he maintained a strong interest in Indian Muslim politics, always taking care never to stray too far from British policy. Jinnah, more aligned to the alternative narrative, described the Muslim League demand for separate electorates as 'dividing the nation against itself'[2]. In 1916, Jinnah played a leading role in forging a pact between Congress and the Muslim League, which was widely recognised as the solution Indian politics had been waiting for. His moment seemed to have arrived.

It was also the year when Gandhi, who had already seeped into the Indian political consciousness because of his heroic triumph in South Africa, began his work on a quiet note for the liberation of India from its many forms of oppression. Foreign rule was only one of them.

Gandhi sailed on the *Kilfauns Castle* from Cape Town on 18 July 1914 for India, via London, where he hoped to meet his mentor, Gopal Krishna Gokhale, who was then on a visit to Europe. He travelled third class and lived purely on nuts and fruits, of which the captain, in honour of his celebrated passenger, ensured a healthy supply. Two days before he landed at Southampton, the First World War broke out. On 8 August, local luminaries were invited to felicitate the hero of South Africa at a reception in the Cecil Hotel. Jinnah was among them. It was their first meeting.

Gandhi tried to do his bit for the war, offering to help with ambulance work on the battlefields of France '...to improve my status and that of my people throughout the British Empire'[3], as he recalls in his autobiography. The goodwill evaporated when Gandhi found Indians would have to take orders from fresh Oxbridge graduates. The British government was if anything relieved when Gandhi left for India on 19 December by the *Arabia*, this time travelling second class because no third-class seat was available. He reached Bombay on 9 January 1915.

The felicitations continued. At a reception in the dazzling splendour of Jehangir Petit's[4] palatial residence in Bombay, Gandhi recalls that he was out of his element after having entered the world of the poor. A separate function was organised by Gujaratis. Gandhi writes, 'Mr Jinnah was present, being a Gujarati, I forget whether as President or as the principal speaker. He made a short and sweet little speech in English.'[5] Most of the others used English as well. Gandhi decided to put his diffidence aside and speak up—in and for Gujarati—protesting against the use of English in a Gujarati gathering.

For a year Gandhi kept a low profile, following Gokhale's advice to keep his mouth shut and his eyes and ears open. Gokhale was quizzical about some of the ideas, if not the idealism, in Gandhi's first political tract, *Hind Swaraj,* written within a week in November 1909 while Gandhi was travelling from London to South Africa. Gokhale told Gandhi to study the India he intended to lead.

In 1917, Gandhi changed the dynamics of Indian politics with his first Satyagraha, on behalf of impoverished and mercilessly exploited peasants of the indigo plantations in Champaran, Bihar. Over the next fifteen years, Gandhi became the central pivot and dominant presence of the nationalist movement, pushing a range of stalwarts into the margins.

Jinnah, unwilling or unable to play second or perhaps third fiddle to Gandhi, first distanced himself from, and then left, the Congress. Instead, he turned his energies towards the Muslim

League. But he had little success in this community clubhouse either. By 1931, after twists, sidesteps, slips and spells of inertia, Jinnah became so frustrated that he shifted home and practice from Bombay to London. In the winter of 1932, he was shocked to learn that he had not been invited to the Third Round Table Conference in London, which gave Muslims one-third representation at the federal level, 51% of the seats in Punjab and just under 50% in Bengal. In 1934, a depressed Jinnah was persuaded to return from London's dead end to revive a now dormant Muslim League. The League, however, did not live up to its own expectations in the 1937 elections. Jinnah was willing to join a coalition government with Congress in the United Provinces. But when Congress, on Nehru's insistence, refused to share power, a livid Jinnah decided that the moment had come to spin the Muslim League into another orbit: first, acute belligerence, and then separation.

Jinnah did not blame Nehru, whom he dismissed as a 'Peter Pan'. His ire was reserved for Gandhi. M.C. Chagla, a professional and political colleague of Jinnah until the latter swerved towards Islamism, has analysed the Gandhi-Jinnah relationship thus:

> Jinnah's besetting fault was his obsessive egoism. He had to be a leader, and the prime mover in whatever cause he worked. With the emergence of Gandhiji in Indian politics, Jinnah felt that his importance would gradually diminish. Jinnah was the complete antithesis of Gandhiji. While Gandhiji believed in religion, in abstract moral values, in non-violence, Jinnah only believed in hard practical politics. Even sartorially it was impossible for Jinnah to subscribe to Gandhi's views. He could not possibly give up his faultlessly tailored suits and his high collars for the simple *khadi*[6] which Gandhiji wanted.[7]

Chagla described Jinnah as '...a poor lawyer but a superb advocate', brilliant at cross-examination. Jinnah used these forensic skills to great effect as he sought to persuade Muslims that their future lay not in Gandhi's platform of unity but on his plank of separation. Gandhi wanted the British to leave, immediately; Jinnah wanted the British to stay until they had delivered his dream. Gandhi believed that the British were responsible for an artificial divide between Hindus and Muslims; Jinnah looked upon the British as an instrument of Muslim salvation. Gandhi reduced himself to poverty; he spent as much time as he could among the indigent and the ostracised. Jinnah was physically averse to even touching the poor.

For Gandhi, religion was an intensely personal and eternal truth whose virtues could be used to improve if not cleanse public life. For Jinnah, religion was a political invention to suit formidable objectives, whose ritual requirements he observed very occasionally, and very hesitantly, to advance a public persona. Not a day passed without Gandhi at prayer. No one recalls seeing Jinnah read the Quran with a believer's devotion. Gandhi believed in a minimalist diet and fasting. Jinnah was an epicure, who liked a good whiskey, believed in quality cooks, fine cutlery and a dining space fit for Western aristocracy.

Gandhi called himself an Advaitic Hindu, one who believed in the philosophy of Sankaracharya that the apparent is an illusion (or *maya*), which separates us from the eternal truth; that God is truth and the way towards truth is non-violence; that Satyagraha is the highest form of political action. Jinnah dismissed this as Hindu revivalism. Is there something to be read in the fact that Gandhi's last words, as he fell from an assassin's bullets, were 'Rama… Rama…'[8], and Jinnah's last word, according to his beloved sister Fatima, who lived with him till the end, was a half-whispered 'Fati...'? Perhaps both, in their last moments, remembered that which mattered most to them: for Gandhi, God; for Jinnah, his sister.

Jinnah was famous for his fiscal honesty, but in his politics he did not let facts interfere with his taunts and tirades.[9] For instance, in December 1938, at the annual session of the Muslim League in Patna, Jinnah described Congress as a fascist Hindu body and Gandhi as its evil genius.

> Who is the genius behind it? Mr Gandhi. I have no hesitation in saying that it is Mr Gandhi who is destroying the ideal with which the Congress was started. He is the one man responsible for turning the Congress into an instrument for the revival of Hinduism. His ideal is to revive the Hindu religion and establish Hindu Raj in this country.[10]

It was a charge so manifestly untrue that it amounted to slander.

An exchange of letters between Gandhi and Jinnah in 1937–38 speaks of an abiding commitment to Hindu–Muslim unity on one side, and a new politics on the other. Gandhi wrote to Jinnah on 19 October 1937, just after the twenty-fifth Muslim League session at Lucknow:

> Dear Friend: I carefully went through your speech at Lucknow, and I felt deeply hurt over your misunderstanding of my attitude... the whole of your speech is a declaration of war. Only I had hoped you would reserve poor me as a bridge between the two. I see that you want no bridge. I am sorry. Only it takes two to make a quarrel. You won't find me one, even if I cannot become a peace-maker. This is not for publication, unless you desire it. It is written in all good faith and out of an anguished heart.[11]

Jinnah replied that it was not a declaration of war, but purely self-defence, and advised Gandhi to read the speech again. Gandhi was ill; but more than that, contemplative before he sent a reply on 3 February 1938. This time it was to 'Dear Mr Jinnah' rather than to a 'Friend'. Gandhi wrote:

> ...You seem to deny that your speech was a declaration of war, but your later pronouncements too confirm the first impression.... In your speeches I miss the old nationalist. When in 1915 I returned from the self-imposed exile in South Africa, everybody spoke of you as one of the staunchest of nationalists and the hope of both Hindus and Mussalmans [sic]. Are you still the same Mr Jinnah?[12]

Jinnah, never to be outdone, answered:

> I would not like to say what people spoke of you in 1915, and what they speak and they think of you today. Nationalism is not the monopoly of any single individual. In these days it is very difficult to define it, but I do not wish to pursue this line of controversy any further.[13]

It may have been difficult to define then, but Jinnah was pursuing a different kind of nationalism even as he wrote those words. These letters did lead to a meeting between the two on 28 April 1938 at Jinnah's residence in Bombay, but their minds could no longer meet.

Jinnah began in his speeches to exploit Gandhi's metaphorical nomenclature, 'Ramarajya', as evidence of the 'Hindu Raj' that Muslims should dread. He scorned Gandhi's talk of harmony as the hypocrisy of a 'Bania'[14] who had found a clever way to keep Muslims in perpetual servitude.

For Gandhi, faith was synthesis. 'Rama is not known by only a thousand names. His names are innumerable, and He is the same whether we call Him Allah, Khuda, Rahim, Razaak, the Bread-giver, or any name that comes from the heart of a true devotee.'[15] When Gandhi added the *Sura al Fateha* to his ashram prayers, 'an ardent Hindu friend' reproached him for killing Hinduism. Gandhi replied that his Hinduism and that of other ashram Hindus had grown by the addition of this beautiful verse, and Hinduism would be enriched by the study of the Quran. Gandhi believed that there could be no independence without the 'mingling' of Hindu–Muslim hearts. Jinnah was equally sure that any peace was possible only after a communal fracture of India.

In the dubious logic of imagined alienation, democracy itself became part of this 'Hindu Raj' conspiracy. Muslims, Jinnah told both the people and the government, would always be 'outvoted' three-to-one in any adult franchise election since they constituted only a quarter of the population, as if Hindu and Muslim voters were perennial religious herds. But the political battle is fought in the court of public opinion. Public opinion does not necessarily seek reason over emotion.

Jinnah's consequent argument, which he developed in well-paced stages, was that Hindus and Muslims were so completely different that they constituted separate nations. Since there was nothing in the past, either political or social, to justify such a conjecture, he concentrated on creating horror stories about a nebulous future. When 'Hindus' took over from the British, they would not merely subjugate Muslims, they would eliminate Islam itself from the subcontinent. He revived the slogan, 'Islam in danger!' Jinnah proved that if Gandhi could integrate religious morality into a vision of future harmony, he could fuse religious rhetoric with fear to mince centuries of coexistence and create a Muslim Pakistan. This was the antithesis of Gandhi's thesis.

TOWARDS PAKISTAN, VIA A VICEROY

On 23 March 1940, Jinnah split the framework of Indian aspirations by asking for a second kind of freedom: a separate state for India's Muslims.

Earlier that month, the 62-year-old Jinnah took a train from Bombay, where he lived in his palatial mansion on Malabar Hill, to Delhi, where he had bought a residence at 10 Aurangzeb Road. He was accompanied by his sister and home keeper, Fatima. His destination was Lahore, for the annual session of the Muslim League. But before he kept his date with history, he had a deal to make in Delhi.

Jinnah developed a slight fever on the train, writes his biographer, Stanley Wolpert.[16] After dinner, as he lay on his berth, he suddenly gasped and moaned, and was in so much pain that he could barely speak. His face was contorted. The next morning his doctor diagnosed pleurisy and advised a fortnight's rest. But Jinnah was up in two days, he could not afford to rest. He had an appointment to keep with the viceroy of India.

Jinnah met the marquess of Linlithgow, viceroy, governor-general and crown representative of His Majesty King George VI on 13 March 1940, ten days before he made a formal demand for Pakistan at the Muslim League session in Lahore. Britain was at a nervous moment in the Second World War. Adolf Hitler's ascendance was in plain sight. Britain needed all the help it could get from India, its most fertile source for men and material.

The bargain was simple. Jinnah offered Muslim support to the British war effort. Linlithgow, in return, gave an undertaking that there would be no settlement on the future structure of India without the concurrence of Muslims. When Jinnah spoke of Muslims, he meant the Muslim League; and when he mentioned the Muslim League, he meant himself.

Jinnah's lifeline to the British was in sharp contrast to Gandhi, who decided that freedom came first. In September 1939, British India declared war on Germany. Gandhi demanded immediate independence in return for immediate support. As he put it later, India was not at war; her conquerors were. Rejecting the advice, albeit subdued, of compatriots like Maulana Abul Kalam Azad and disciples like Jawaharlal Nehru, Gandhi forced provincial Congress governments elected in 1937 to resign and declared that India would support the Allies only as a free nation, not as a colony. From London's perspective, war was not a time for negotiations, especially those that left Britain looking weak and the Empire wobbly.

Gandhi's stance was not without its contradictions. In 1914, he had argued that England's need should not be turned into India's opportunity, and even went out of his way to recruit volunteers for the British Army, exhorting bewildered Gujarati peasants to prove to sceptical Englishmen that they could become lions on the battlefield. His hope then was that Britain would show its gratitude through greater self-government for India after the war. Instead, Britain tightened its imperial grip after victory in 1918. Gandhi was not ready to trust Britain a second time.

He had often felt betrayed. In 1899, during the Boer War in South Africa, he raised a 1,200-strong ambulance corps from the Indian community. In 1906, he led stretcher bearers to nurse Africans wounded in the battles against Zulus, as whites were reluctant to touch blacks. Each time, his help had been accepted during conflict and forgotten once the shooting stopped.

From the British perspective, in 1940, Jinnah offered soldiers and Gandhi offered grating advice, some of it laced with convoluted views on non-violence that befuddled wartime British officials. On 26 May 1940, Gandhi suggested to Linlithgow in a letter, 'I do not believe Herr Hitler to be as bad as he is portrayed. He might even have been a friendly power as he may still be.' He offered to go to '...Germany or anywhere to plead for peace ... for the good of mankind'[17]. The viceroy sent a cool response: the war would continue till victory. The British never forgot Jinnah's help, nor forgave Gandhi's hostility.

Statistics will underline just how important Jinnah was to Britain during this existential conflict. At the start of the Second World War, the Indian Army numbered 205,000 men. By 1 January 1941, this had doubled to 418,000. Of this, 155,000, or 37 per cent, were Muslims. Nearly half of the total army, or 201,000 men, came from Punjab, which then stretched from the edge of Delhi to the Hindu Kush, and about half of these Punjabi recruits were Muslims. There were 51,000 Sikhs and 46,000 Gurkhas from Nepal. Compared to this, only 63,000 men came from regions where Congress was strong, such as Bombay, Central Provinces, United Provinces and Bihar. Of these, 18,700 came from a traditional source, the Mahrattas.[18]

The demands of the bloodiest war in history would multiply the need. At the height of conflict, over 2.5 million Indians were fighting for Britain, the largest volunteer force in history. Desperate, the Raj abandoned its practise of recruiting mainly from what it called the 'martial races' of India and took on all comers. But the major catchment region was still Punjab. Indian troops fought in Europe, Malaya, Singapore, Egypt, Libya, Iraq, Syria, Persia, Somaliland, Abyssinia and Burma.

The deal done, Jinnah reached Lahore by the Frontier Mail on the morning of 22 March 1940. There was rapturous applause from roughly 60,000 Muslim League delegates as he reached the dais. Two thrones were placed on the stage, a large one for him and a smaller one for his sister. He had changed from his Western suits to the more domestic long coat, the achkan and narrow pyjamas. He spoke for two hours in English, a language that not too many of the delegates understood. He had only one message for Gandhi: the Mahatma should come, proudly, as a Hindu leader and meet him as the leader of Muslims. 'The Mussulmans are not a minority,' he asserted. 'The Mussulmans are a nation by any definition.'[19] If the British were sincere about the happiness of Indians, they would divide India into 'autonomous national States'. He did not use the word 'Pakistan' in either his speech or the resolution passed by acclamation the next day, but left no doubt that he was demanding a sovereign Muslim state.

Congress had prepared for such an eventuality by naming its own pre-eminent Muslim leader, Maulana Abul Kalam Azad, as its president. The Congress session, also in March 1940, was held in Ramgarh. Azad, in his presidential speech, delivered in fine Urdu, dwelt on the indivisible place of Muslims in the history and culture of India. Of critical relevance was the Congress resolution on the war. It said that:

> [Britain was fighting] fundamentally for imperialist ends and for the preservation and strengthening of her Empire, which is based on the exploitation of the people of India, as well as other Asiatic and African countries.... The Congress therefore strongly disapproves of Indian troops being made to fight for Great Britain and of the drain from India of men and material for the purpose of the War.

In an attempt to weaken the case for a two-nation theory, Congress said that:

> [N]o permanent solution is possible except through a Constituent Assembly, where the rights of all recognised

> minorities will be fully protected.... India's Constitution must be based on independence, democracy and national unity, and the Congress repudiates attempts to divide India or to split up her nationhood.

Gandhi was baffled by Jinnah's suggestion that he reinvent himself as a leader of only Hindus and the demand for a separate state for Muslims. He wrote in the 30 March 1940 edition of his journal, *Harijan*:

> I am proud of being a Hindu, but I have never gone to anybody as a Hindu to secure Hindu–Muslim unity. My Hinduism demands no pacts.... I am no politician in the accepted sense. But whatever talks I had with Quaid-e-Azam or any other have been on behalf of Congress which is not a Hindu organization.

He added pointedly that the '50,000' delegates at the League session could not claim to represent eighty million Indian Muslims. The following week, in the 6 April edition of *Harijan*, he sharpened his response:

> I do not believe that Muslims, when it comes to a matter of actual decision, will ever want vivisection. Their good sense will prevent them. Their self-interest will deter them. Their religion will forbid the obvious suicide which partition would mean. The 'two-nations theory' is an untruth. The vast majority of Muslims of India are converts to Islam or are descendants of converts. They did not become a separate nation as soon as they became converts. A Bengali Muslim speaks the same tongue that a Bengali Hindu does, eats the same food, has the same amusement as his Hindu neighbour.

Gandhi asked Jinnah whether his surname was Hindu or Muslim.

> For his name could be that of any Hindu. When I first met him, I did not know that he was a Muslim. I came to know his religion when I had his full name given to me. His nationality was written on his face and manner. The reader will be surprised

> to know that for days, if not months, I used to think of the late Vithalbhai Patel as a Muslim as he used to sport a beard and a Turkish cap.... Sir Mohammed Iqbal used to speak with pride about his Brahmanical descent. Iqbal and Kitchlew are names common to Hindus and Muslims. Hindus and Muslims of India are not two nations. Those whom God has made one, man will never be able to divide.[20]

This is as close to getting publicly angry as Gandhi ever got.

Jinnah was indifferent. The only reassurance he needed was from the British. By the time he met Linlithgow in late June, any doubts or misgivings about this historic bargain had disappeared. Britain was in the gloom of its darkest hour. Hitler, already master of Poland, smashed through Denmark and Norway in April 1940. In May, it was the turn of Belgium, Netherlands, Luxembourg and France. Between 27 May and 4 June, British forces barely managed to escape from Dunkirk. On 22 June, France surrendered. America's President Franklin Roosevelt was sympathetic, but Americans were not yet willing to join a European war. Britain stood alone. India's men and money were essential to its faltering war capacity. Jinnah was the only Indian politician of any weight, ready and able, to support Britain. There was little point in being ready to help, as Nehru was, but unable to do anything about it.

Stanley Wolpert describes this June meeting thus:

> Jinnah visited the viceregal palace at Simla on June 27, 1940, conferring at length with Linlithgow. Afterwards he wrote a memo reaffirming that the Lahore 'Pakistan' resolution had become 'the universal faith of Muslim India' and that the viceroy had promised him 'that no interim or final scheme of new constitution would be adopted by the British Government without the previous approval of Muslim India.' They had also agreed that 'everything should be done that is possible to intensify war efforts and mobilise all the resources of India for her defence for the purpose of maintaining internal security, peace and tranquillity, and to ward off external aggression'.[21]

Gandhi, in contrast, seemed to have lost the plot as far as the war was concerned. He wanted the British to become the ultimate Satyagrahis, abandon an 'undignified competition in slaughter' and hand over their country and colonies—including presumably India—to Hitler and Mussolini. On 2 July 1940, he wrote an open appeal 'To Every Briton':

> I venture to present you with a nobler and a braver way, worthy of the bravest soldier. I want you to fight Nazism without arms, or, if I am to retain the military terminology, with non-violent arms. I would like you to lay down the arms you have as being useless for saving you or humanity. You will invite Herr Hitler and Signor Mussolini to take what they want of the countries you call your possessions. Let them take possession of your beautiful island, with your many beautiful buildings. You will give all these, but neither your souls, nor your minds. If these gentlemen choose to occupy your homes, you will vacate them. If they do not give free passage out, you will allow yourself, man, woman and child, to be slaughtered, but you will refuse to owe allegiance to them.[22]

Gandhi then offered his personal services to the viceroy to help the British purify their souls and abandon their imperial possessions.

As if a public exhortation was not enough, Gandhi visited Linlithgow to repeat the suggestion. The viceroy, says Azad in his memoir, was so bewildered that he forgot his usual courtesies. At the end of a conversation, he would normally ring the bell for someone to escort Gandhi to his car; this time, he quite forgot to do so and Gandhi had to find his own way out.

The British elite still took pride in a stiff upper lip, but we can imagine their sneer when that upper lip relaxed. On 24 December 1940, Gandhi appealed to the Fuehrer through a letter to adopt non-violence. It began by saying that Gandhi personally did not believe Hitler to be a monster, but some of his acts were indeed monstrous. The bulk of this epistle dwelt on how non-violence would end British rule in India.

> In non-violent technique, as I have said, there is no such thing as defeat. It is all 'do or die' without killing or hurting. It can be used practically without money and obviously without the aid of the science of destruction which you have brought to such perfection. It is a marvel to me that you do not see that it is nobody's monopoly. If not the British, some other power will certainly improve upon your method and beat you with your own weapon.[23]

He wanted Hitler to stop the war and refer all disputes to an international tribunal. The letter, intercepted by the British censors, never reached Hitler.

Gandhi could find unusual ways to irritate the British. In a 'purely personal letter' to Linlithgow on 26 July 1940, he took umbrage at

> [Money] being spent like water in the name of war. Men who have enjoyed fat salaries in their respective jobs are being taken up for the war at much higher salaries and given ranks to which they have never been used before. The largest number of these are said to be Europeans or Anglo-Indians.[24]

Such suggestions were unlikely to impress the Raj.

On 8 August 1940, Linlithgow publicly confirmed what he had assured Jinnah privately. Titled 'The August Offer' and 'issued with the authority of His Majesty's Government', this core commitment would not waver over the next seven years. The viceroy, praising India's 'mighty contribution' in the 'world struggle against tyranny and aggression', and 'anxiety' to increase this aid, reiterated the old assurance of Dominion status after the war. The new assurance was to those making a substantial part of the contribution, the minorities. It clarified all doubts as to '…whether the position of minorities, whether political or religious, is sufficiently safeguarded in relation to any future constitutional change by assurances already given.' It went on to say:

> The first is as to the position of minorities in relation to any future constitutional scheme.... His Majesty's Government's concern that full weight should be given to the views of minorities in any revision has also been brought out. That remains the position of His Majesty's Government. It goes without saying that they could not contemplate transfer of their present responsibilities for the peace and welfare of India to any system of government whose authority is directly denied by large and powerful elements in India's national life. Nor could they be parties to the coercion of such elements into submission to such a Government.[25]

On 21 August 1940, Gandhi sent a draft for the Congress Working Committee response to this 'Viceregal pronouncement' from his ashram in Wardha. He called it 'highly unsatisfactory and provocative'. Congress, he said, was the only non-communal, non-sectional and wholly democratic organisation, and would sweep elections in every province under adult franchise.

> What the British government have done is to play the Muslims against the Hindus and vice versa in order to consolidate their power and to exploit the vast resources of India in their own interest. It is they who finally cut the nation in twain by introducing the virus of separate electorates. The Congress therefore repudiates the British claim specially to represent Muslim interests in so far as they may be in danger from the Hindu majority. The Congress has claimed that the political and economic state of both is identical. The Congress has undertaken to guarantee to the full the protection of the religious and cultural rights of Muslims.[26]

Jinnah, reassured by 'The August Offer', kept up his drumbeat for separation, lest anyone forget, and asked a party colleague, Shah Nawaz Khan, to prepare a blueprint for a future Pakistan, which he received in February 1941. This report persuaded Jinnah that it was impractical to expect the whole of Punjab and Bengal and he realised, privately, that a partition of these provinces would be necessary if his project was to become a reality. East

Punjab had a non-Muslim majority, while only 54.8% of Bengal was Muslim.

Jinnah now sought to expand his influence among Muslims in South India, where he had thus far little visibility. The 1941 session of the Muslim League was scheduled for 12 April in Madras. On the train, Jinnah collapsed again with fever and pain. The local doctor called it a nervous breakdown, but Jinnah and his sister knew that an irreversible tuberculosis was eating away his life. Jinnah often told colleagues that he would continue his quest for Pakistan even if it killed him. An unspoken question hovered over his destiny. Would his health fail before his Pakistan succeeded?

JINNAH'S TRUMP CARD

By the winter of 1941, Jinnah's investment in the British war effort began to pay off in ways no one could have envisaged in March 1940.

The high drama of Pearl Harbour on 7 December 1941 has tended to obscure the spectacular success of Japanese forces from the Pacific to the South China Sea, Bay of Bengal and the Indian Ocean. Japan's military discipline was extraordinary: the Pearl Harbour task force that left in late November moved in such radio silence that it could not be detected by radio traffic analysis. One person, however, was quietly relieved. Churchill had expected a Japanese onslaught on British possessions in South East Asia. Pearl Harbour was a double bonus, for America had been dragged into war. That night, famously, Churchill 'slept the sleep of the saved and thankful'.

The bliss evaporated very quickly. Japan had moved not only towards Hawai, but also towards South East Asia. On 8 December, Japan's 18th Division brushed aside heavy seas and defensive fire to take Kota Bharu in the north of Malaya. British forces fled, leaving four bases intact for the Japanese to capture. By 13 December, some 1,500 Japanese troops, accompanied by one tank company, had destroyed the 14,000-strong 11th Indian Division at Jitra. Details of the fighting need not detain us, but in fifty-five days, Japan took Malaya and Hong Kong, although the island fortress of Singapore still held out.

Japan bombed Singapore on the day it landed in Malaya, 8 December. On 9 December, the pride of the British fleet, the *Prince of Wales* and *Repulse*, were sunk off its coast. On 16 December, the Japanese bombed Rangoon. On 20 January 1941, while Wavell was reading Churchill's 'absolutely clear' order that every inch of ground had to be defended, the Japanese incursion into Burma began. On 15 February, the much-vaunted and reinforced 60,000-strong British-Commonwealth garrison at Singapore surrendered, virtually without firing a shot. Churchill's orders had again been explicit: officers 'should die with their troops' in defence of the honour of the British Empire; instead they melted and disappeared. Around 7,000 of the 12,000 Australian troops deserted. The percentage was higher among Indians. Japan took over 80,000 prisoners.

On 8 March, Rangoon fell. By 23 March, Japan had occupied a part of India, the Andaman Islands, which took its advance to within a hundred-odd nautical miles of Indonesia. On 5, 6 and 9 April, Japan's air force and navy bombarded Colombo, Vishakhapatnam, Coconada (on the east coast of India) and Trincommallee (in Sri Lanka). On 9 April, the Americans withdrew from Bataan. The Japanese seemed invincible as they set up their Asian empire, euphemistically described as the 'Greater East Asia Co-Prosperity Sphere'.

The British completed their retreat on 10 May 1942, just two days before the onslaught of the monsoon would have turned jungles into swamps and rivers into torrents. Statistics do not always tell the full story, but these do. In Burma alone, the Empire lost 13,463 men, including prisoners of war, of which 4,033 were killed or wounded. In Malaya and Singapore, the number was 138,708, of whom 94 per cent surrendered, many of them preferring to do so as an escape from the horrific misjudgements of generals. Japan lost only 5,500 lives while routing Britain from the Far East.